Poems for a Winter Afternoon

By Patrick Meighan

Poems for a Winter Afternoon

By Patrick Meighan

Published by Unsolicited Press
Portland, Oregon
www.unsolicitedpress.com

Copyright © 2018 Patrick Meighan
All Rights Reserved.

No part of this book may be reproduced or transmitted in any form or by any means without written permission from the publisher or author.

For information, contact the publisher at info@unsolicitedpress.com

Unsolicited Press Books are distributed to the trade by Ingram.
Printed in the United States of America.
ISBN: 978-1-947021-70-9

Contents

Steppes	9
Dear Anna	10
Feast for Flies	11
Exile From Your Eyes	12
Stray Dog Cafe	13
Old Dogs	14
Dusk Scene	15
Credal	16
To Brigit at Imbolc	17
Death Under Ice	18
After the Ice Storm	19
Poems for a Winter Afternoon	20
February Stains	24
El Campo	25
Solst/Ice	27
Companions	28

To the many teachers/poets who have inspired me.

Steppes

Death everywhere,
Yet so many empty graves.
Not even the snow can fill them.

Dear Anna

The news is not good. The world has grown a bushy mustache. In this epoch, people shiver in long lines uncertain where they lead. I don't think even you could describe it. Grim men in gray suits have replaced soldiers. They carry smartphones. Everyone seeks out his own lies. This morning was so cold when I awoke. Outside my window a pine tree uprooted by the winter hurricane leans toward your Russia, where you left some wine and crumbs of bread. Last night in a dream I spoke with Osip. We waited for you in an old century, but you didn't show. Only the century came, but it soon grew sentimental. Osip said he misses you. A New World Order sends its love.

Feast for Flies

Alone at a long table
A feast for a king has been
Set before you and before
The empty seats. The untouched
Food is cold. This dining room
Is a memory, but not a memory.
The lights are low. You are dead.
My thoughts are dead.
The only sound the distant
Buzzing of flies coming from
Inside you, inside me,
From these lines,
This decomposition.

Exile From Your Eyes

It's as if the winter lasted one hundred years
And I was banished to the North
Where the blizzard stings my eyelids,
As if to blind the memory of your eyes,
Astonishingly clear and glacial.
You once walked barefoot through melting snow
For me, your bared breasts like new suns.
But that seems a thousand springs ago.
Today I light the wood stove.
Inside, I burn memories like witches.

Stray Dog Cafe

After Osip Mandelstam

I think of Saint Petersburg and crave to share
A tavern meal surrounded by friends and poets.
Yes, a little something to eat, maybe just a morsel.
Venison would be nice, washed down with wine.
Svetlana will pour what I like: dark, very dry, light
On spice. I will eat and drink robustly and invite
You to do the same on a night for warm fires,
For cleavage to soften the eyes. Outside, wind
Will blow harshly. Winter is getting a late start.
Outside, I am unhappy. I will curse the scalawags
For what's theirs. Inside there – which is nowhere,
But still beloved – her green eyes will recite verses
She adores. Me? I will eat and then drink more
For joy's sake in the velvet of a night so pure.

Old Dogs

A wind in an overcoat
Fills the river's trousers
On the line of shore's oily sheen.

And you, whom I loved, but hate?
Your eyes,
Yes, your blue eyes, which
Were never kind
Are icy castles
Now
Cold, and chaste.

Cold? Yes, the cold aches
And trees are barren except for a few leaves
That linger, land-locked syllables
Of half-forgotten lies. Old dogs growl at ghosts
Who ceased to care

But care, but cease to
See whether the lies they had lived
Live still. They live.

Dusk Scene

An ambulance passes a field with a single tree.
The siren fills its empty branches.
In moments the echo dissolves.
All soon will be swallowed by torrential darkness.
And drowned within one silent, barren tree.

Credal

My cat slays religion in the backyard,
Stalking chipmunks in vestal robes
Among tiger lilies and ornamental grass.

She gives up the Holy Ghost
In sleek fur vomited,
The tiniest gnashed bones
In which God dwells.

And I bear witness
To systems of faith destroyed.

I forsake the village hound barking
At the moon that shines on churchyard graves,
Or chimes ringing in an empty church
Among shadows cast by saints
Painted onto dusty windowpanes.

For my cat is a spirit
Slaying rodent theocracies
Among the ornamental grass!

To Brigit at Imbolc

It's a cold moon, Brigit.
Soon, the ewes lactate.
Such sweet milk will fatten
The Easter lambs.
There is feast in sacrifice.
I, an old believer who has spoken
Prayers through this winter
And set aside my crumbs,
Now would knead your flesh –
Body and blood you gave us –
Like dough for bread.
Snow is on the ground, Brigit.
Trees wave bony fingers
At my dark window.
I await your ladies to
Dance the world into blossom.
Wind you say will carry owl songs.
Now it still grows dark early,
The fire is cold ash at dawn.
Yet you promise Spring
When the dough will rise.

Death Under Ice

Searching for a break, a hole,
A fissure to punch through,
A man spiders across
The underside of a frozen pond.

Though he moves like a spider,
He is a fly caught in a web
Of ice and water,
With Death closing in.

An opaque ceiling above,
Darkness below. As he crawls
Everything is radiant
With silence.

After the Ice Storm

After Charles Simic

This is what I saw – trees like crystal mummies,
Wrens picking over the glazed grass littered
With razor shards that broke off branches,
And my neighbor on his knees chipping ice off
His front steps.

He was a Michelangelo cursing god and his muse,
Feverishly freeing a figure of stone from ice,
Flecks of ice like marble in his beard
While the cold sun was having a good laugh
At his expense.

Poems for a Winter Afternoon

i.

"These are dark and evil days,"
Said the cat at her window perch.
"Snowflakes scurry like mice.
The wind hounds me all afternoon."

ii.

A man near the window,
Branches of a silver maple
Scraping against it.
Somewhere down the hall
A cat scratches at a door.

iii.

O prophecy!
At the wood's edge
A witch walks through snow
Leaving bird tracks.
A black cat pads behind.

iv.

Sign: "Because of weather,
The soup kitchen is closed.
We will reopen at dinner tomorrow."
One man stood in the blizzard
Peering in. From the dark inside
A tabby on break from mouse patrol
Sat peering out into the settling dusk.
The street was empty except for wind
And snow and dark mounds of buried
Cars. And one man and one cat
Whose eyes met only in dreams.

February Stains

Today the wind is stealing newspapers.
Schoolboys short-cut through the Jewish
    Cemetery,
Trip into pre-dug graves of the still-living.
A diner faces the wasted winter streets.
Inside, low conversation from a TV set. Old goats
At the counter graze on eggs and hash. Swill coffee
In buckets, bleat "hun" at the waitress.
February drips away. The season's music sings
In grease stains on old coats, a smeared score,
Its notes dripping discordantly toward March.
Winter has stained the waitress's face, though in
    jeans
Her figure still turns heads. The old goats scratch
At beards and dream of young legs gamboling.
Outside, schoolboys clamber from empty, frozen
    graves.

El Campo

Night falling fast
Across the vast sky.
Two dogs and the flock
Descend into this valley,
A Wyoming meadow.

A tin camper.
Inside, Heriberto,
A Peruvian sheepherder,
Huddles over beans and rice
Cooking on a Sterno.

Behind his closed eyes
Andean loneliness dissolves.
He forgets the coyotes, the blizzards,
The impossibility of sheep.

Week after week he has for companions
One snarling dog who is the devil,
Another steadfast as the frost.

He dreams each night of Norita
Waiting at a dusty threshold. Her hands
Blooming with flowers.

And in this cold hour, when the earth
Smells of human dust and is in this gloom,
I want to rap on all the doors
And beg, I don't know whom, for pardon,
And bake him fresh bits of bread
Here, in the oven of my heart.

(Italic lines are translated from the Spanish of Cesar Vallejo by P.M.)

Solst/Ice

Ghosts
Of a thought
The darkening river
Swallows its rocks
A precip/ice
Of violence
The sun dies
Of avar/ice

Companions

Two skeletons clear the parking lot
Of the remains of a half Nor'easter's
Wind-driven sleety stew.
Thus one never feels alone, even in partial
        whiteness
And no wind to cool the sweating bones
In skein of overcoats and woolen skull caps.
Blessed always are the dead.

Acknowledgments

Thanks to the editors of the journals in which these poems have appeared:

Abalone Ink: The translated lines of "El Campo," which appeared in a translation of the Cesar Vallejo poem "El Pan Nuestro."

Alexandria Quarterly Magazine: "Exile From Your Eyes"

Convivium: "El Campo," "To Brigit at Imbolc"

Inflectionist Review: "Feast for Flies"

Red River Review: "After the Ice Storm"

Wilderness House Literary Review: "Old Dogs," "Credal," "Poems for a Winter Afternoon"

About the Author

A former newspaper reporter, Patrick Meighan now lives the life of a nomadic adjunct professor, teaching poetry, composition, literature, and journalism courses at several four-year and two-year colleges. His poems, book reviews, and translations have appeared in many online and print journals. He earned his MFA in poetry from the low-residency program at New England College. He resides in Manchester, N.H.

About the Press

Unsolicited Press started without the bootstraps in California in 2012, and has progressed to publish out-of-this-world fiction, creative nonfiction, and poetry. Now based in Oregon, the team refuses to accept industry standards and acquires quirky, phenomenal, and true art from authors around the world. Learn more at www.unsolicitedpress.com.

www.ingramcontent.com/pod-product-compliance
Lightning Source LLC
Chambersburg PA
CBHW030136100526
44591CB00009B/684